SCIENCE SECRETS

SECRETS OF
HEAT
AND COLD

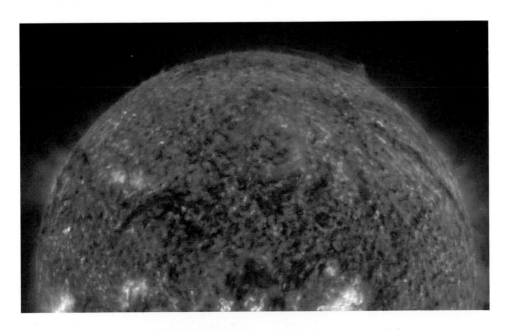

ANDREW SOLWAY

W

This paperback edition published in 2014

First published in 2010 by Franklin Watts

Franklin Watts
338 Euston Road
London NW1 3BH

Franklin Watts Australia
Level 17/207 Kent Street, Sydney NSW 2000

Produced by Arcturus Publishing Limited,
26/27 Bickels Yard, 151–153 Bermondsey Street, London SE1 3HA

Planned and produced by Discovery Books Ltd, 2 College Street, Ludlow, Shropshire SY8 1AN, www.discoverybooks.net
Managing editor: Paul Humphrey
Editor: Clare Hibbert
Designer: sprout.uk.com limited
Illustrator: Stefan Chabluk
Picture researcher: Sabrina Crewe

Photo acknowledgements: Corbis: pp 4 (Caroline), 16 (Michael Benson/Kinetikon Pictures); Getty Images: pp 5 (Visuals Unlimited/Scientifica), 25 (Visuals Unlimited/Scientifica), 29b (Koichi Kamoshida); IStockphoto: cover polar bear (John Pitcher); NASA: p 23 (NASA Dryden Flight Research Center Photo Collection); Science Photo Library: pp 8bl (Mitsuo Ohtsuki), 10br (Tony McConnell), 19 (Edward Kinsman), 20 (Crown Copyright/Health & Safety Laboratory), 27 (Paul Rapson); Shutterstock Images: cover frost (ElenArtFoto), cover and pp 1 sun (Ekaterina Starshaya), 6 (Amra Pasic), 7 (Fotocrisis), 8r (thumb), 10tr (jathys), 11 (CSLD), 15 (akva), 17 (Andraž Cerar), 18 (Armin Rose), 21 (Wojciech Zbieg), 24 (Joe Belanger), 26 (Matka Wariatka), 29t (Daisy Daisy); US Geological Survey: p 14 (R.L. Christiansen).

Words in **bold** type appear in the glossary on pages 30–31.

A CIP catalogue record for this book is available from the British Library.

Dewey Decimal Classification Number 536.5

ISBN 978 1 4451 3119 1

Printed in China

Franklin Watts is a division of Hachette Children's Books, an Hachette UK company.
www.hachette.co.uk

SL001239EN

Supplier 03, Date 1113, Print Run 3058

Contents

Why are heat and cold important?

We need heat for so many things in our lives. Do you start the day with a warm shower? The shower water has to be heated. If you have toast for breakfast, you need heat to make it. If you travel to school by car or bus, the engine needs heat to work.

These examples are just the beginning of the story. Most **electricity** is made in **power stations** that run on heat.

▼ *In a blast furnace, iron ore is heated until the iron is molten. It can then be separated from the solid slag (waste).*

Using heat

Metals must be heated to get them out of the rocks where they are found. Plastics are made from oil – a process that uses lots of heat. Even this book needed heat to make it. The paper is made from wood that was 'cooked' in water and chemicals.

Cooling down

Heat is not always useful. Sometimes we need to cool things down. Fridges and freezers keep food cold, so it lasts longer without going bad. Fridges in hospitals keep medicines and **vaccines** fresh.

Many engines and machines have to be cooled, or they overheat and do not work properly. Even people need cooling! We sweat to stay cool in hot weather.

Studying heat and cold

In this book you will learn some of the amazing things scientists have found out about heat and cold.

▲ *A **thermogram** is a special picture that shows how much heat an object or living thing gives off. Hot areas appear red or yellow; colder areas green or blue.*

Humans are warmer than their surroundings, because **mammals** generate heat inside their bodies. Our bodies produce surprising amounts of heat. In just 15 minutes, an adult gives off enough heat to boil a litre (more than 2 pints) of water! A young person, being smaller, gives off less heat.

What are heat and cold?

Heat is a kind of **energy** – scientists call it **thermal energy**. The hotter something is, the more thermal energy it has. The boiling water used to make a cup of coffee has a lot more thermal energy than cold water from the tap.

Cold by comparison

It sounds strange, but cold and heat are the same thing! Something that is cold has thermal energy, as does a hot thing. Something is only hot or cold compared to something else.

When we talk about things being hot or cold, we usually mean compared to our bodies. An ice cube feels cold because it is colder than the body.

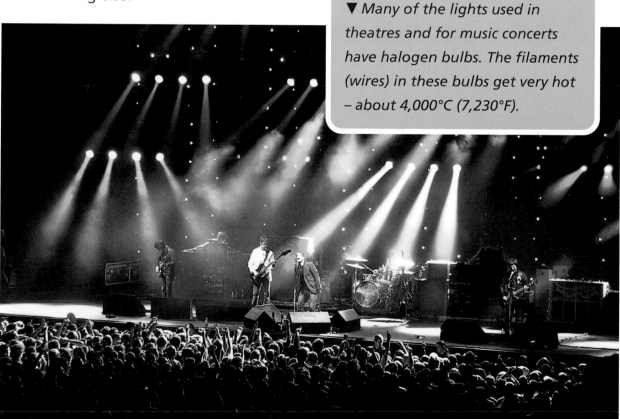

▼ *Many of the lights used in theatres and for music concerts have halogen bulbs. The filaments (wires) in these bulbs get very hot – about 4,000°C (7,230°F).*

A cup of coffee feels hot because it is warmer than the body.

However, if you compared a cup of coffee to a pot of molten iron, you could say that the coffee is relatively cold – the molten iron is far hotter.

▶ An ice cream is 'cold', but in fact it still has a lot of thermal (heat) energy.

EXPERIMENT

TRICKING THE SENSES

This experiment demonstrates how our senses can be confused about whether something is hot or cold.

You will need:
• a glass of iced water (take the ice out after cooling the water)
• a glass of hand-hot water • a glass of water at room temperature

1. Put the first finger of your right hand in the glass of hot water, and the first finger of your left hand in the cold water. Leave them there for about a minute.

2. Now put both fingers in the room-temperature water. Do the fingers feel the same, or different?

How is a hot spoon different from a cold one?

You can't tell if a spoon is hot or cold by looking at it. You have to touch it to find out. So how *is* a hot spoon different from a cold one?

Moving particles

You can only see the differences between a hot and a cold spoon using a powerful microscope. Like everything else in the universe, a spoon is made up of billions of incredibly small **particles**.

▼ *Some microscopes are so powerful that they can actually show the particles that make up matter. This picture shows particles of solid uranium.*

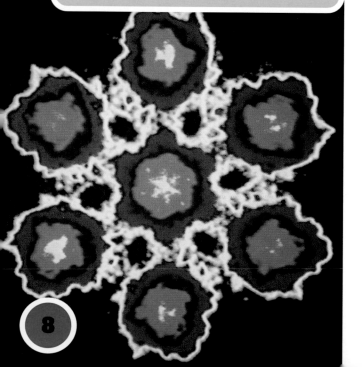

Solids...

In a solid material, the particles are packed close together. The particles are not still – they constantly **vibrate**, like people jostling in a crowd. The movement (**kinetic energy**) of the spoon's particles is thermal energy. As the spoon gets hotter, the particles vibrate more strongly, jostling each other more and more.

▶ *Is this spoon hot or cold? We cannot tell simply by looking at it.*

Liquids...

The particles in a liquid are further apart than those in a solid. They jostle each other less frequently than in a solid, because they have more space to move about. This is why a liquid flows and doesn't keep its shape.

... And gases

In a gas, the particles are much further apart. They are like people running around in a big field, rather than being crowded together. The particles move faster and further than in a liquid, and only occasionally collide (bump into each other). This is why gases can expand to fill a space.

SCIENCE SECRETS

THE ELEMENT OF HEAT

Today we take it for granted that heat is energy. But for years scientists thought that heat was a substance, like air or water.

In 1789 Anton Lavoisier, the French scientist known as the 'father of chemistry', put together the first list of chemical **elements**. One of the elements on his list was 'caloric' – heat.

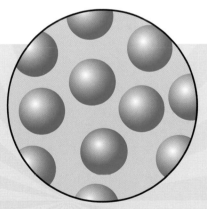

In a liquid, the particles jostle each other and move about.

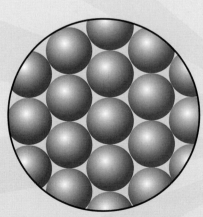

In a solid, the particles vibrate but stay in one place.

In a gas, the particles are far apart and travel quickly.

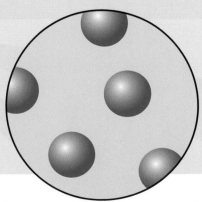

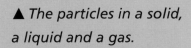

▲ *The particles in a solid, a liquid and a gas.*

Why does hot chocolate go cold?

Your hot chocolate is too hot to drink so you leave it to cool for a few minutes. While you are waiting, you start reading a book. Suddenly you remember your drink and take a sip. Oh, no – it's cold! What happened to all that heat?

Heat flow

Heat does not always stay in one place – it can move around. However, heat always flows in one direction: from a hotter region to a colder one. Your hot chocolate goes cold because heat flows out of the drink and into the surrounding air.

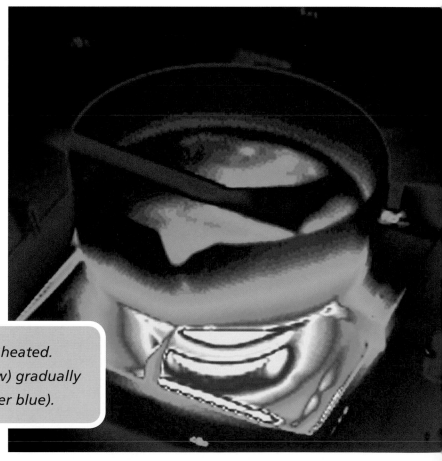

▶ *A thermogram of water being heated. The hot gas flame (red and yellow) gradually transfers heat to the water (lighter blue).*

What about cold things?

When you take an ice cube out of the freezer, heat flows the opposite way. The ice cube is colder than the air around it, so heat flows into the ice cube from its surroundings. The result is that the ice cube melts.

Both the hot chocolate and the ice cube end up being the same temperature as their surroundings.

▼ *A geyser is a jet of boiling hot water gushing out of the ground. The water is heated by molten rocks deep underground.*

SUN AND EARTH

The sun is immensely hot (see page 16) – far hotter than anything else nearby. So heat flows out from the sun into the surrounding space. This is very lucky for us. Without the heat flow from the sun, earth would be a dead planet.

There is another, smaller heat flow on earth – from the centre of the earth to the surface. Billions of years ago, when earth first formed, it was so hot that the rocks were molten. The surface gradually cooled, but the planet's **core** is still very hot. Heat constantly flows from the core towards the surface.

How can heat be transferred?

Heat can move from place to place in different ways. How it moves depends on whether it is passing through a solid, a liquid, a gas – or nothing at all!

Heating a poker

If you put one end of a poker in a fire, that end gets hot. The particles in the poker vibrate much more when they are hot. As they vibrate, they bump into other particles close to them, and pass on some of their energy. Gradually, heat passes up the poker as the particles pass on energy through many collisions. This kind of heat transfer is called **conduction**. It only happens in solids.

▲ *If you put a poker or an iron bar in a fire, heat slowly travels up the metal by conduction.*

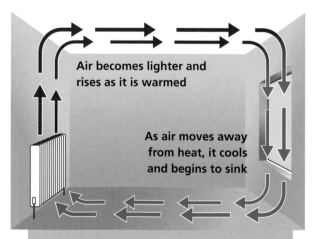

Air becomes lighter and rises as it is warmed

As air moves away from heat, it cools and begins to sink

▲ *A radiator warms a space mainly by convection – the movement of air around the room.*

Warming a room

If you have a fire or radiator in a room, it warms the space mainly by **convection**. Air close to the fire or radiator soon gets warm. The warm air expands, because the gas particles in it are moving faster. The air particles are now spread out, so the air is lighter. This lighter air rises.

As it does so, cooler air flows in to take its place. Soon all the air in the room is flowing in a circle: warming near the fire, rising, then cooling and sinking as it moves away from the heat.

Radiating out

Heat can move in a third way, known as **radiation**. This is when heat travels as invisible rays called **infrared** waves.

Radiation can travel through a **vacuum** (empty space). This is the way that heat from the sun reaches us.

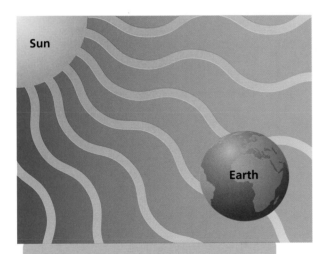

▲ Heat from the sun reaches earth by radiation. This is the only way that heat can travel through a vacuum (empty space) because there are no particles to move the heat energy by conduction or convection.

EXPERIMENT

MOVING IN CIRCLES

This experiment shows how convection moves a liquid or gas.

You will need:
• a clear bowl • some warm water • a small jug of cold water • ice cubes • food dye

1. Put some warm water in the bowl.

2. Chill the water in the jug with ice, then add some food dye to the water.

3. Now add one drop of the dyed water to the bowl of warm water. Watch what happens to the dye. The heat of the water swirls it by convection.

Is heat the same as temperature?

The temperature of an object is a measure of how hot or cold it is. However, this is not the same as the amount of heat (thermal energy) it contains.

For example, the filament (wire) in an electric light bulb reaches a temperature of 3,000°C (5,530°F) when the light is on. However, the filament does not store much thermal energy, so it cools down quickly when the light is turned off.

▼ *A scientist measures the temperature of hot lava at Mauna Ulu, a volcano on Hawaii.*

By contrast, an iceberg is at a much lower temperature of 0°C (32°F), but it can store much more thermal energy. It takes huge amounts of energy to raise the iceberg's temperature by even 1°C (around 2°F).

Heat capacity

The scientific measurement of how much heat a substance can store is called **heat capacity**. To measure the heat capacity of an iceberg and a light filament, scientists take the same weight – usually 1 g (0.04 oz) of water (for the iceberg) and tungsten (for the light filament) – and see how much energy it takes to raise the temperature of each substance by 1°C (around 2°F). Water has a much higher heat capacity than tungsten, and it takes longer to heat up or to cool down.

▲ *A traditional adobe house has thick walls with a high heat capacity. This helps to keep the interior cool during the day.*

TESTING HEAT CAPACITY

This experiment uses fire. Be careful, use common sense and ask an adult to help you.

You will need:
• several balloons • a night light and matches • water

1. Blow up a balloon and tie it off. Put the night light in the sink and light it. Ask the adult to move the balloon over the flame (not too close). What happens? It bursts!

2. Carefully fill another balloon about a third full with water, blow in a little air and tie it off.

3. Relight the night light, and ask the adult to hold the second balloon over the flame. What happens? The second balloon does not pop. Water has a high heat capacity so it 'soaks up' heat from the flame and stops the balloon from overheating.

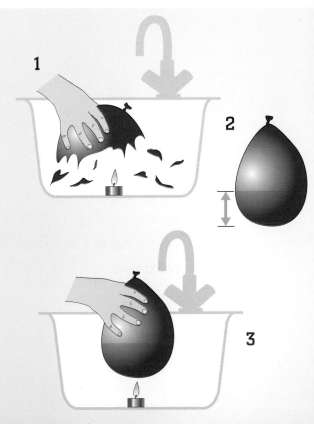

What are the hottest and coldest things there are?

The hottest and coldest things we know about are not on earth. Out in space, there are things that are much hotter and colder than anything on our planet.

The heart of the sun

Our sun is very hot – the surface temperature is almost 6,000°C (10,830°F). That's three or four times hotter than a steel furnace. However, this is nothing compared to the temperature at the sun's core – 15.5 million°C (28 million°F)!

The sun is only one of trillions of stars in the universe. Some of the largest, hottest stars have core temperatures of 100 million°C (180 million°F). But even this is not the hottest thing we know. At the end of its life, a large star dies in a huge explosion called a **supernova**. Temperatures in a supernova can reach 100 billion°C (180 billion°F)!

The coldest places

Away from the heat of the sun or other stars, space is very cold. In fact, empty space is the coldest thing we know. The temperature can reach –270°C (–454°F). This is three times colder than the lowest temperature ever recorded in the Antarctic, –88°C (–126°F).

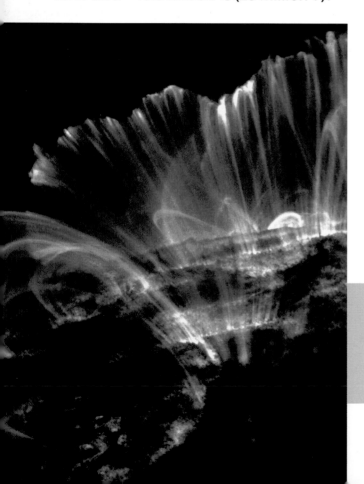

◄ *The sun's surface is a swirling mass of extremely hot gases. Some parts are hotter than others, and sometimes huge flares burst out from the surface.*

SUPER HOT

In 2006, scientists in New Mexico, USA, raised the temperature of a cloud of **charged particles** to a temperature of 2 billion°C (3.6 billion°F). This is over 100 times hotter than the cores of the biggest, hottest stars.

Absolute zero

The hottest known temperature is much more extreme than the coldest. This is because there is a limit to how cold something can become.

As the temperature gets colder and colder, the particles in a substance move less and less. At −273°C (−460°F), a temperature known as **absolute zero**, the particles have no heat energy. This is the coldest possible temperature. Scientists have managed to artificially cool material to within a ten-billionth of a degree of absolute zero.

▶ The gas **nitrogen** becomes liquid at −196°C (−321°F). This is very cold, but still well above absolute zero (−273°C, −460°F).

How do animals keep warm?

Cold weather is dangerous for animals. If an animal gets too cold, it may die. An animal's body is made up of tiny cells, which are mostly water. If the water freezes, it damages the cells. So how do animals stay warm in cold weather?

Insulation

One important way of keeping warm is through **insulation**. An insulator is a material that stops heat from flowing easily through it. A bird's feathers are very good insulators.

Most mammals have fur or hair for insulation. Whales, seals and other sea mammals have a layer of fat under the skin, called blubber, instead. Blubber is a better insulator in water than fur or feathers.

▶ *Weddell seals are the only mammals that live in Antarctica all year round. They survive because of their thick layer of blubber (fat).*

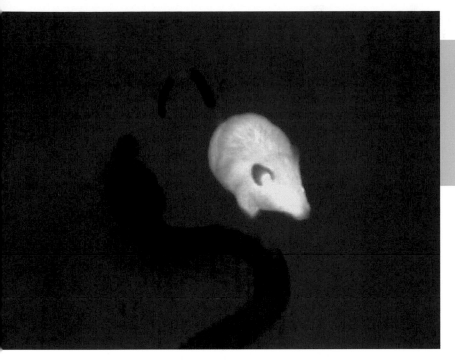

◄ *The snake in this thermogram is not much warmer than its surroundings, but the mouse can keep warm even in a cold environment.*

Varying temperature

Reptiles do not have an insulating layer. At night, or in cold weather, reptiles often burrow underground. The ground is a good insulator, and so the temperature below ground does not fall as low as at the surface.

In the morning, reptiles have cooled down so much that they are sluggish. They 'sunbathe', or bask in the sun, to warm up their bodies.

Warm-blooded

Mammals and birds are **warm-blooded**. This means that they can stay warm, even in cold weather. Insulation helps, but mammals and birds also need to eat and digest food to produce heat and to stay warm. Warm-blooded animals need to eat more than animals such as reptiles, whose body temperature can vary.

SCIENCE SECRETS

NATURAL ANTIFREEZE

Fish and insects are like reptiles: in cold conditions, their bodies get cold, too. In very cold weather, the water in their bodies could freeze. To stop this from happening, fish and insects that live in cold places have special **proteins** in their bodies, called antifreeze proteins. These proteins stop ice from forming inside their bodies.

How can we produce heat?

We saw at the beginning of the book that we use heat for many different purposes, from heating houses to powering aircraft. How do we produce all of this heat?

Combustion

We get most of the heat we need by **combustion** (burning **fuel**). It is a **chemical reaction**, in which fuel (the substance being burned) reacts chemically with oxygen from the air. This reaction happens very fast and produces large amounts of heat.

Most fuels are substances that were once living things. Wood was the main fuel that humans used in the past. Today the most important fuels are coal, gas and petroleum (oil). These are the remains of animals and plants that lived millions of years ago.

Friction

When you rub two surfaces together, it produces heat. If you rub the palms of your hands together, they quickly start to feel warm. This is heat produced by **friction**.

Friction can produce unwanted heat. The brakes on bicycles, cars and trucks work by friction. If they are used a lot, they can overheat. Truck brakes have to be specially cooled to prevent overheating.

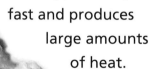

◄ *Fuels must be stored with care, because they burn so easily. In 2005, there was a serious accident when oil storage tanks at Buncefield, UK, caught fire.*

► *A worker uses a grinder to cut metal. The friction produces sparks.*

TESTING COMBUSTION

This experiment tests whether oxygen is needed for combustion. You will need an adult helper.

You will need:
• a small candle • a jar
• sticky tack • bicarbonate
of soda • vinegar

1. Put a bit of sticky tack on the base of the candle, then stand it in the jar. Spread bicarbonate of soda around it.

2. Light the candle: does it burn well?

3. Now pour a small amount of vinegar on the bicarbonate of soda.

4. When bicarbonate of soda and vinegar mix, they react chemically to produce **carbon dioxide** gas. This fills the jar and pushes out the air. The candle flame is starved of oxygen, and so it goes out.

How do we make heat work for us?

Producing heat by combustion is one thing. But how do we turn this heat into useful work? One way is to make a **heat engine**.

What is a heat engine?

Heat engines burn fuel to produce movement. Cars, trains, aircraft, ships and most power stations are powered by heat engines.

▼ *A car engine works in four stages. The power stroke (stage 3) produces enough power to push the crankshaft through two complete cycles.*

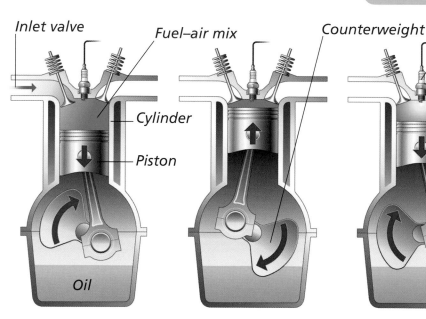

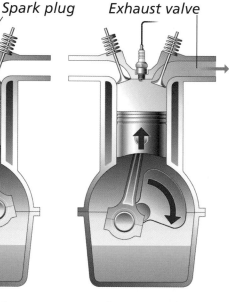

Inlet valve   *Fuel–air mix*   *Counterweight*   *Spark plug*   *Exhaust valve*

Cylinder

Piston

Oil

1. Intake stroke: air and fuel are drawn into the cylinder of the engine as the piston moves down.

2. Compression stroke: the counter-weight helps the piston to rise again and squash the fuel–air mix.

3. Power stroke: the spark plug lights the fuel, which produces hot gases that push down the piston.

4. Exhaust stroke: the burned fuel is released from the cylinder, through the exhaust valve.

The most important part of a heat engine is the **working fluid** – a liquid or gas (usually water or air) that is heated by the burning fuel. As the working fluid gets hot, it expands (takes up more space). The expansion of the working fluid produces movement.

Different kinds of engine

In petrol and diesel engines, fuel and air burn inside a **closed cylinder**. One end of this cylinder is a piston, which can slide up and down. The hot, expanding air pushes the piston and drives the engine.

Most aircraft are powered by **jet engines**. In a jet engine, air and fuel explode in a **combustion chamber**. The hot, expanding gases are channelled out through a nozzle. This produces a powerful jet of gases that drive the aircraft forward.

Steam **turbines** are engines used in many power stations and some ships. The working fluid is water, which is heated and turns into steam. The steam drives many-bladed fans called turbines, which spin round and power an electric **generator**.

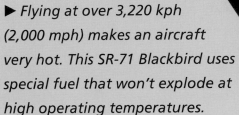

▶ *Flying at over 3,220 kph (2,000 mph) makes an aircraft very hot. This SR-71 Blackbird uses special fuel that won't explode at high operating temperatures.*

ELECTRICITY FROM HEAT

A thermoelectric generator (TEG) is a new kind of 'engine' that produces electricity directly from heat. It contains two special metals, and produces electricity when one metal is heated and the other is kept cool. Some car makers have built experimental cars with a TEG fitted to the exhaust. It produces enough electricity to reduce the car's fuel consumption by 5 per cent.

What happens when substances melt or boil?

We cook food in boiling water because, once it is boiling, the water does not get any hotter. It stays at 100°C (212°F) even though the water is still being heated. What happens to all the heat?

Changing into steam

When water boils, it begins to **evaporate** (change from a liquid to a gas). This process uses a lot of energy. The heat energy being added to the water makes it evaporate rather than making it hotter.

Melting solids

Something similar happens when a solid melts and becomes a liquid. If you put an ice cube in a warm room, it absorbs heat from the surrounding air. This heat energy makes the ice melt. Until it melts, the ice does not get warmer: it stays at 0°C (32°F).

Condensing and freezing

When a gas cools enough to **condense** (become a liquid), or a liquid begins to freeze, the process releases energy. When you want to make ice cubes, for example, you have to keep removing heat from around the water. That's because heat energy is released as the ice forms.

◄ The bubbles in boiling water are water that has turned to vapour (gas) that then rises out of the liquid.

▲ A thermogram of an ice cube. The solid ice (purple) stays at 0°C (32°F). Once it melts (pink, yellow), the water warms up until it is the same temperature as its surroundings.

KEEPING DRINKS COOL

This experiment shows why we use ice to cool drinks in hot weather.

You will need:
- ice cubes • two glasses
- water • a thermometer

1. Fill each glass with water and add some ice cubes to each one.

2. Keep checking the temperature of the water in each glass with the thermometer. When it reaches 0°C (32°F), add some more ice to both glasses.

3. Leave one glass at room temperature and stand the second glass in a bowl of hot water.

4. Measure the temperature of the water in each glass every few minutes until the ice melts. What do you find? You should find that the water in both glasses stays at around 0°C (32°F) until the ice has melted. However, the ice in the second glass (in hot water) melts faster.

How does a refrigerator keep things cool?

A fridge relies on the fact that a liquid needs heat in order to evaporate (turn into a gas).

What happens in a fridge?

A refrigerator has a set of pipes that run round the inside. A pump pushes a liquid that boils at a low temperature through the pipes.

Inside the fridge, the pipes suddenly change from being narrow to wide. This gives the liquid space to expand, and it evaporates. The liquid gets the energy it needs to change into a gas from its surroundings. This cools down the air inside the fridge.

From gas to liquid

For the fridge to keep working, the process has to keep on happening, so the gas in the fridge pipes has to be turned back into a liquid.

This happens on the outside of the fridge (usually at the back). The gas is squeezed into smaller pipes and turns back into a liquid. As it does so, it gives out heat, which is released into the air. When you feel the air behind a fridge, it is warm.

▲ *When food is kept in a fridge, the chemical reactions that make it spoil are slowed down. This keeps the food fresh.*

HEAT PIPES

Heat pipes are amazing devices that soak up heat in one place and move it somewhere else to be absorbed by a **heat sink** (a substance with a high heat capacity). They are thin metal tubes that have no air inside, but contain a small amount of liquid. Heat moves very quickly from the warmer end of the pipe to the cooler end, without the need for a pump or other moving parts.

Heat pipes are used in some solar heating panels (panels that use the sun to heat water), and to cool high-performance computers. The latest heat pipes are as thin as a credit card.

▼ A heat pipe helps cool a computer by carrying heat away from the electronic parts to a heat sink.

What happens when things get really cold?

Fridges are not only used for cooling food. Scientists use special refrigeration units in their laboratories.

At very low temperatures, gases such as oxygen and nitrogen condense and become liquids. Liquid nitrogen is used as a low-temperature coolant to preserve blood and other living materials for medical use.

Strange behaviour

Some materials do odd things at low temperatures. At around –271 °C (–456 °F), two degrees above absolute zero (see page 17), the gas helium becomes a **superfluid**. A superfluid acts mostly like a liquid, but if it is put in a container it moves up and spills over the top of the container.

Superconductors

At very low temperatures, some materials become **superconductors**. They conduct electricity brilliantly and can make extremely powerful **electromagnets**. These kinds of magnets are used in **MRI** scanners, which take detailed pictures of the inside of the

SUPER SLOW

In 1999 scientists at Harvard, USA, made a superfluid called a Bose–Einstein condensate. In this material all the individual particles were packed together so closely that they behaved as if they were one giant particle. Light shone through this material travelled about 20 million times slower than its normal speed! In another experiment in 2001, the material briefly stopped the light from a laser.

body, and to power some high-speed trains. Scientists investigating the structure of atoms use superconducting magnets in huge machines called particle accelerators. These accelerators smash tiny particles together at high speeds.

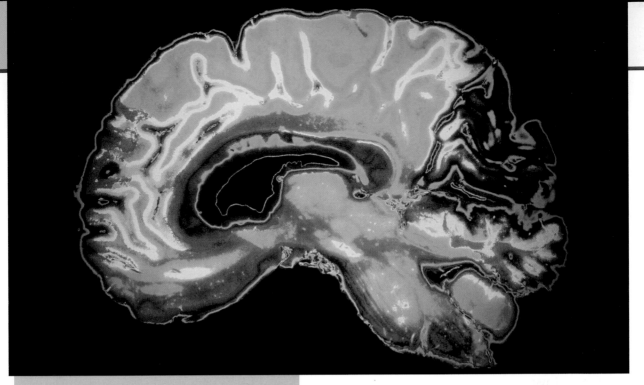

▲ *An MRI scan of a human brain. The electromagnet at the heart of the scanner has superconducting wires.*

▼ *This Japanese **maglev** train uses superconducting magnets. In test runs it has reached over 580 kph (360 mph).*

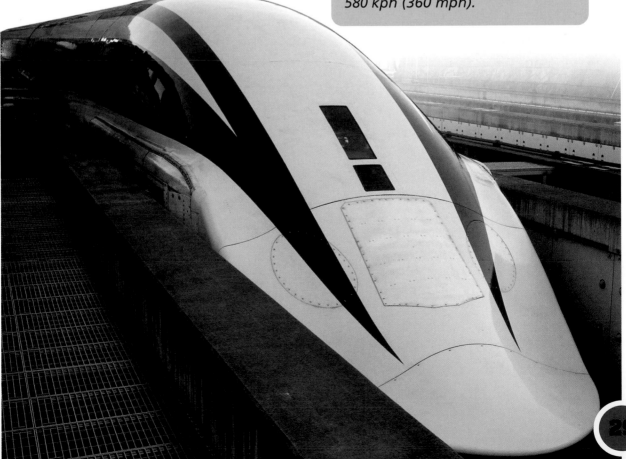

Glossary

absolute zero The coldest possible temperature, at which the particles in matter have zero energy and cease to move.

carbon dioxide A gas that makes up a small part of the air and does not support combustion.

charged particles Some of the tiny particles that make up everything can have a positive or negative electric charge. They are charged particles.

chemical reaction A process in which a substance or substances are changed chemically (become different substances). This is different from a physical reaction, such as melting or freezing, where the substance involved remains the same chemically.

closed cylinder A tin can shape, closed at each end.

combustion The chemical reaction of burning.

combustion chamber The part of a jet or other engine in which the fuel is burned.

condense To change from a gas into a liquid.

conduction The way that heat moves through a solid, in which the particles in the solid pass energy on by bumping into each other.

convection The way that heat moves through a fluid (liquid or gas), in which the heat spreads in a circulating flow.

core The central part of something, such as a planet. Earth's core is very hot, made mostly of molten iron.

electricity A form of energy produced by the movement of electrons (extremely tiny charged particles).

electromagnet A magnet produced by passing electricity through a coil of wire.

element A simple chemical that is made up of just one kind of atom.

energy The ability to do work or make changes happen.

evaporate To change from a liquid into a gas.

friction A force that slows down objects when they rub against each other, or when they move through a fluid.

fuel Something that burns to produce lots of heat.

generator A machine that produces electricity.

heat capacity Scientifically called specific heat capacity, the amount of energy needed to raise the temperature of a specific weight of a substance by 1°C (around 2°F).

heat engine A petrol, diesel or jet engine, or any other engine that is powered by burning fuel.

heat sink A piece of material with a high heat capacity that stores and releases heat slowly.

infrared A kind of radiation similar to light rays, which conveys heat.

insulation A way of reducing the flow of heat from place to place, for example by using a material that stops heat flow.

jet engine An engine that burns fuel to produce a hot jet of gases.

kinetic energy The energy of movement.

maglev Short for magnetic levitation. Describes an object that is lifted from the ground by magnetic force. Maglev trains run at high speeds, because they are not slowed down by the friction of having contact with the ground.

mammal An animal that is warm-blooded, usually has a furry or hairy coat and feeds its young on milk. Humans, horses and mice are all mammals.

MRI Short for Magnetic Resonance Imaging. A technique that uses invisible waves, which react to a magnetic field, to view the body's organs.

nitrogen An inert (unreactive) gas that makes up four-fifths of the air.

particle One of the tiny pieces (atoms) that make up all the matter (all substances) in the universe.

power station A factory that generates large amounts of electricity.

protein A natural substance found in all animals and plants that is essential for living processes.

radiation The transmission of energy by rays similar to those of light. Heat radiation is transmitted by infrared rays.

superconductor A material that, at low temperatures, conducts electricity so well that virtually no energy is lost.

superfluid A gas or liquid that, at very low temperatures, flows without friction.

supernova An immense explosion that marks the end of the life of a very large star.

thermal energy The energy of heat.

thermogram A special kind of photograph that uses different colours to show how hot or cold an object is.

turbine A propeller or fan with two or more blades that turns when a gas or liquid flows through it.

vaccine A substance given to someone that makes their body think it has got a particular disease. This helps the body fight off the real disease if it ever gets infected.

vacuum Empty space.

vibrate To wobble or shake.

warm-blooded Describes animals that can produce heat inside their bodies to keep them warmer than their surroundings.

working fluid A gas or a liquid that expands and contracts within an engine to make it work.

Further information

Books
Horrible Science: Killer Energy by Nick Arnold and Tony de Saulles (Scholastic Children's Books, 2009)

Internet-linked Library of Science: Forces, Energy and Motion by Alastair Smith (Usborne Publishing, 2001)

Science Files: Heat and Energy by Steve Parker (Heinemann Library, 2004)

Science Lab: Experiments with Heat by Trevor Cook (Franklin Watts, 2009)

Websites
Animated Engines (www.animatedengines.com) *Watch the workings of internal combustion (car) engines, steam engines and other kinds of heat engine.*

BBC Science and Nature: the Sun (www.bbc.co.uk/science/space/solarsystem/sun) *Take a tour around the sun and learn some amazing things about the star that supplies nearly all the earth's heat.*

Nova: Absolute Zero (www.pbs.org/wgbh/nova/zero/about) *What is cold, how do you make things cold, and how cold can it get? Find out all about it on this website.*

Shanghai Maglev Train (www.smtdc.com/en/gycf.asp) *The website of the world's first high-speed maglev train.*

Index